Unsung

Niesha Steinke

BookLeaf Publishing

Presentation by *BookLeaf Publishing*

Web: www.bookleafpub.com

E-mail: info@bookleafpub.com

ISBN: 9789357212502

First edition 2023

DEDICATION

For my mother, the English teacher, who
instilled in me a love of words and writing.

PREFACE

"There is a song in my heart that no one can sing but myself. I can't force you to listen, but i am responsible for the music I make." - @oxherdboy

For a long time, I have not given myself permission to sing my song. However, during my Sabbatical, it has felt like an important form of soul care to engage my creativity and allow my voice to be heard. I invite you to pull back the curtain and listen with me.

Obsession

On the highway of my mind
the path is well worn
no directions needed
to that destination
deeply known
and yet unbidden.

Blind

It's no small thing
to be mistaken for someone else
judged for what you didn't say
rather than what you did.

Do I try to defend myself?
Do I set the record straight?

No.

It's not my job to force your eyes open
when you choose
what you want to see.

Forgotten

If all that's left is
an empty space
        on the email signature line
an empty office
        with an unused gray couch
an empty fridge
        without my stack of lunch containers
an empty seat
        at the meeting table
Will your heart soon be empty
        of the space it held for me?
Will I be forgotten?

Another Look at Lot's Wife

She gets a bad rap
Lot's wife (like most women I suppose)
Was she so salty about leaving
her bougie urban life
that she had to take one last look?

Or was she slow to release the heart-strings
that tied her to all she knew and loved?
Her friends, her family, her home…

Enrobed in salt
her tears memorialized.
Why is it so hard to let go?

Enough

The need to create
bursts through my body in ways
that I can't ignore

Is this real sickness
or is it a heavy weight
of feelings and pain

both mine and others
none of which I can resolve
only acknowledge

For today
that is enough.

Survivor

Symbol of peace
How many lives have you lived?
Choked almost to death
Extremities blackened
Ripped to unrecognizable
Blown to shreds
Uprooted and pulled apart
Yet holding on
You continue to bloom
Your strength, unimaginable
Your legend, irrefutable
Survivor.

Escaping Egypt

Racing mind
anxious heart
constricted muscles
throbbing head

If freedom feels so foreign
no wonder they longed for
the familiarity
of bondage.

Good Enough

In the classroom confessional
similar stories brought forth
the struggle to be perfect was real.
Though pardonable, this ancient passion
was still a sin to be overcome.

Shocked and silent, I listened to one
who had never succumbed to
this inhuman pressure.
How did she do it?

A maternal gift in a mantra:
"Better is the enemy of good enough."

The First Step

The first step is the hardest
chubby dimpled feet
extend from their comfortable curled
position
the effort of coordinated movement
heavy lifting
searching for that point of solid
connection
and then the cheering and clapping
celebration all around
affirmation of the feat accomplished.

The first step is the hardest
standing stories high
keeping company with clouds and
treetops
the gap enormous between
the cable thin as thread
to bear the weight
of all you carry
when finally you let go
and soar through the air
free, victorious, triumphant.

The first step is the hardest
accepting your limitations and
shortcomings
facing a different direction
from that which gave you worth
to seek healing, clarity and purpose.
You only see dimly
as in a fog
but you have befriended fear before

Brave soul,
the first
is always
the hardest.
Trust.

Hibernate

Why envy the poor lot who
perennially waste
          their time, their life
          dormant, listless, trapped
opportunities and seasons
passing them by.

What is the function of this design?
to do nothing
but rest

Safe, warm, cozy, secure

Is it not a return to the womb?
Is it not a chance to be born again?

Deep Roots

Rooted and grounded in love
such an eloquent turn of phrase

But what they didn't tell us
is that the breaking of the seed
the pushing through the hard shell
the feeling your way through the darkness
it is not easy.

Growth hurts, that is the plain truth
and you feel like you are searching
searching
searching
for a drop of water to quench your thirst.
Down you go, deeper still
until

One drop is all you can handle at first
but you soak it up, soak it in, soak in it

The time of refreshing has come
From the stream of living water
and you receive the longed-for nourishment
and you look around and discover
the vast network of strength, connections and
possibilities
that were created in your darkest moments.

Dreamer

When we had company
I disdained sleep
never wanting to miss
the excitement.

If only I knew the nighttime escapades
my imagination had in store
would I hardly deign to keep
their company.

Sabbath Lessons

I.
What if the very first day of the
rest of your life
was that?

Was it not so for Adam and Eve?
No need as yet to tend, cultivate or produce
No wonder it was Paradise.

II.
A whole nation identified as a labor force
"You are what you do."
Took 40 years of desert manna to learn
There is One making provision for you.

III.
Before any
          teaching
                    preaching or
                              healing
the Voice of blessing heard
in being
my beloved.

IV.
In Paradise restored
when we lack nothing
within or without
will we see clearly
and wonder
and worship?

As a Little Child

Let yourself be known
    in unchecked laughter
    in unleashed creativity
    in free-flowing movement
    in hunger, thirst, weariness and need

Let yourself be seen
    in reckless pursuits
    in unrehearsed performances
    in open-mouthed wonder
    in pain, in tears, as a beginner

Let yourself be loved
    in falling or mastery
    in the messiness or the pristine
    in activity or rest
    in every stage of growth

As a little child
    just in being.

Red Panda

Solitary
Elusive
Vulnerable

You live in the shadows of your larger namesake
And though you shun the limelight
You can't help but stand out
Your striking splash of color
Eclipses the black and white

Unique
Original
Enduring
Beautiful.

Motherhood

Sometimes before the day breaks
I find your small body tucked into mine
Little chilled feet
pressed to my legs for warmth
Your small back
tight against my chest
My arm envelops you
I cover your tiny hand with my own
feeling the softness of your skin
I listen to your breathing deepen and slow
bonded on a cellular level
my heart tucked into yours.

Night Watch

Stay close beside me
for a minute more
a little voice called out to me
as I headed for the door.
Let me feel your touch
soft upon my face
your hand steady on my back
my literal safe space.
Even with my eyes closed,
I sense that you are near
your presence brings me comfort
I have nothing to fear.

Christmas Lights

One marvels at the electricity required
Another at the sheer variety:
          Pig in a Santa hat
          Tipsy Daniel Tiger
          “Bah Humbug”
          Red helicopter…Polar express?
          The family favorite –
      an illuminated tree arch
      rainbow colors in neat lines
      symmetrical perfection.
The third sits in rapt attention
eyes twinkling
best lights of the night.

Morning Routine (when you're 4)

An early morning cartoon
Forget Curious George
it's Mickey Mouse
or Doc McStuffins now
A breakfast of chocolate chip waffles
no syrup or butter
maybe some fruit
strawberries if we have them
or pomegranate seeds
Change clothes
PJ's inside out
piled on the floor
Steadied by the familiar
Ready for the day ahead

Calling

What if following your calling
is less about career, vocation, or location?
What if it is being faithful
to who you are
showing up unabashedly
with your unique gifts
in whatever setting you find yourself?
What if it's glorifying God
through being fully alive
and allowing that life
to spark new life in others?
What if you are simply called
to be true to who you were created to be?

www.ingramcontent.com/pod-product-compliance
Lightning Source LLC
Chambersburg PA
CBHW062111140826
49812CB00058B/1248
9789357212502